Hip-Hop Heroes

Raphaella Ramirez

SCHOLASTIC INC.
New York Toronto London Auckland Sydney
Mexico City New Delhi Hong Kong Buenos Aires

Cover photo
© Ebet Roberts

Copyright © 2004 by Scholastic Inc.
All rights reserved. Published by Scholastic Inc.
Printed in the U.S.A.

ISBN 0-439-68625-3

SCHOLASTIC, READ 180, and associated logos and designs are trademarks and/or registered trademarks of Scholastic Inc.

LEXILE is a registered trademark of MetaMetrics, Inc.

5   6   7   8   9   10   23   12 11 10 09

Contents

Introduction

In the 1970s, disco ruled. Disco was dance music. It was on the radio and in the clubs. There were even disco movies.

But disco dancing wasn't cheap. The clubs charged lots of money to get in.

Some kids in New York City didn't have much money. So they started making their own music. They couldn't buy fancy stuff. They had only **turntables** and records.

The kids played for free in local parks.

---

turntables record players

In the 1977 movie *Saturday Night Fever,* John Travolta stars as a guy who loves to disco dance. Here, he's dancing with Karen Lynn Gorney.

They **wired** their turntables to street lamps. All of their friends showed up. And everyone danced.

This new kind of music became known as rap or hip-hop. Here are some of the people who made it famous.

wired hooked up to electricity

*This DJ used two records and a rhyme.
And he made a new sound.*

1

Kool Herc

In the 1970s, a kid named Kool Herc brought a new sound to New York City. Herc grew up in Jamaica. At 13, he moved to New York. He lived in a part of the city called the Bronx.

That was in 1967. A few years later, Herc started going to parties. There, disc jockeys (DJs) would **spin** records. And everybody would dance.

spin to play

Herc loved to dance. But he didn't like the music the DJs were playing. Other Bronx kids wanted better music, too.

So, Herc started buying records. He used them to spin his own music. Then he started to play at parties.

Herc used a trick from Jamaica. He didn't play just one record at a time. He mixed sounds from two records.

Herc knew that kids loved to dance to the breaks. Breaks are long drum parts in the middle of a song. Breaks have no **lyrics**, or words. They just have music.

Herc decided to make the breaks longer. To do this, he used two copies of the same record. He also used two turntables. He'd put each record on its own turntable.

lyrics words to a song

© David Atlas/Retna Ltd.

Kool Herc got his start in the 1970s. Thirty years later, he was still performing. Here he is at Central Park in New York City in 2001.

"I'd find out where the break was," Herc says. First, he'd play the break on one record. Then, he'd play it on the other record. Sometimes he'd do that a few times. That made the breaks really long.

"People loved it!" Herc says.

Herc also talked, or rapped, over the breaks. He knew lots of kids at the parties. When he rapped, he'd shout out to them. He would talk in rhyme. He said things like, "I see . . . Wallace Dee . . . in the house!"

People loved Herc's raps. But soon, Herc was too busy with the turntables. He needed someone else to rap. So he began to work with an MC. The MC rapped. And Herc spun records.

Other DJs saw that people loved Herc's act. So they teamed up with MCs too. They made great music. Rap was born.

Why did kids like Kool Herc's music?

Grandfather of Rap

Rappers love James Brown.

This may surprise you. Rap has roots in church music.

Kool Herc's favorite singer was James Brown. Brown has been popular since the late 1950s. He did not sing in churches. But he used the **rhythms** of church music in his pop songs.

Brown's songs were called "soul music." Often they had long drum breaks. Kool Herc

© David Redfern/Redferns

James Brown, also known as the Godfather of Soul, performs in 1983.

loved to spin Brown's songs. His MCs rapped over the breaks in his songs.

Later, many hip-hop DJs used Brown's music! In fact, rappers still use his music today. That's why Brown is called the Grandfather of Rap.

rhythms the repeated beats in music

Radio stations start playing rap.
And it's a hit across the country!

2

The Sugarhill Gang

At first, hip-hop was just in New York City. And it was just party music. It wasn't on the radio. And you couldn't buy it in stores.

Then Sylvia Robinson came along. Sylvia worked for a record company near New York City. Her kids loved hip-hop. One day, Sylvia had an idea. Her company would make a rap record.

© Janette Beckman/Retna Ltd

© Michael Ochs Archives

The guys above were the Sugarhill Gang.
From left to right, there's Wonder Mike,
Big Bank Hank, and Master Gee.
The group was Sylvia Robinson's idea.
She's to the right.

In 1979, Sylvia brought together three rappers. One was called Wonder Mike. Another was Master Gee. The third rapper was Big Bank Hank. Sylvia called them the Sugarhill Gang.

The Sugarhill Gang made a song for Sylvia's company. They took a break from a disco song. They made up rhymes. And they rapped over the break. The song was called "Rapper's Delight."

Soon, "Rapper's Delight" was on the radio. People loved it! The song played on stations all over the world. And it sold more than two million copies.

The Sugarhill Gang never had another big hit. But they took rap past New York City. And they brought it to people everywhere.

The raps were new.
The flash was too.

3

Grandmaster Flash

It was the early 1980s. A rap group named Grandmaster Flash and the Furious Five were a big hit. They weren't the first group to make it big. But Flash made up some new ways to spin. And his rappers made up new rhymes.

Like Kool Herc, Flash was from the Bronx. Why was he called "Flash"? His hands moved really fast on the turntables.

Grandmaster Flash *(middle)* **and the Furious Five. They are** *(from left to right)* **Melle Mel, Kid Creole, Cowboy, Raheim, and Mr. Ness.**

© Ebet Roberts

Other DJs' music wasn't always smooth. You could tell when they switched turntables. But Flash was different. You could never tell when he switched. His mixes were super smooth.

Flash liked to mix tiny pieces of many songs. He would mix them into one rap single. No DJ had ever done this. Flash called his style *quick mixing.*

Flash also had a new way to make cool rhythms. He would put the needle on the record. Then he would move the record back and forth with his hand. This was called "scratching."

Flash had other tricks, too. He spun records behind his back. He also spun under the table. He was one of the first DJs to do these tricks.

Flash made spinning look easy. But he worked really hard. He practiced at home for a year. Then he started playing at parties.

Flash had an MC called Cowboy. Cowboy made up raps. He'd shout, "Clap your hands to the beat!" Or he'd say, "Wave your hands in the air like you just don't care!"

Those words have been on *lots* of rap records. But Cowboy said them first.

Grandmaster Flash used to hide his records. He didn't want anyone to copy them. But today, his sound and style are all over hip-hop.

B-Boys, Get Down!

Hip-hop fans made up a new way to dance.

"B-boys, get down!"

That's what Kool Herc used to say. He would shout it at the start of a drum break. All the dancers in the room would go wild.

They would get down on the floor. They would spin on their heads, backs, and hands. They would do splits. They would try to make up new moves.

These dancers loved to dance during long drum breaks. So their kind of dancing was called **break dancing**. And kids who did this kind of dance were called b-boys and b-girls.

Break dancers had their own fashion. They wore nylon track suits. The slick suits were good for sliding across the floor. They also wore sneakers with wide laces.

Some break dancers danced in groups. And some of those groups got famous. They danced at big events. They danced in music videos. One group even danced for President Bill Clinton.

break dancing a kind of dancing done during drum breaks

Hip-hop and break dancing spread all over the world. Here's a scene from championships in London, England.

4

Run DMC

By the mid-1980s, hip-hop was on the radio. Stores sold hip-hop records. Still, hip-hop wasn't a big part of the music world. No rapper had ever made a gold record. And no rapper had ever had a video on MTV.

Then a group came along that changed that. The group was called Run DMC. It had three members. Jam Master Jay was the DJ. Run and DMC were the MCs.

Jam Master Jay *(left)* **walks the streets of New York city with Run** *(middle)* **and DMC. Jam Master Jay was killed in 2002.**

The guys put out their first single in 1983. It was called "It's Like That." It was a hit.

In 1984, the band made its first album. Some of the songs didn't just have spinning and rapping. They had live heavy metal guitar music, too.

That was a first for rap artists. And it brought the band new fans. These new fans were rock and metal lovers. They had never liked hip-hop. But now they started listening to Run DMC. Before long, the band's first album went gold!

One song on this album was called "Rock Box." Run DMC made a video for "Rock Box." It was the first rap video on MTV.

In 1986, Run DMC had their biggest success yet. Their third album became the best-selling rap album ever!

One song on this album was called "Walk This Way." It was a remake of a song by the rock band Aerosmith. The two bands did the remake together. It was the first time a rap group and a rock band worked together.

"Walk This Way" was one of the biggest hits of 1986. It was the first rap single to reach the top 10. The video played on MTV almost every hour.

Run DMC had become a super-group. Rap was finally at the top of the charts!

What was new about Run DMC's music?

A girl group makes it big.
And they take a tough stand.

5

Salt-N-Pepa

For years, most people in hip-hop were men. Then a group called Salt-N-Pepa came along. They weren't the first female rap group ever. But they were first to make it big.

Cheryl James was "Salt." Sandra Denton was "Pepa." The two women worked together at Sears. A friend was making a rap record. He asked them to

© Helmut Werb/Retna Ltd.

Salt *(top right)* **and Pepa** *(top left)* **pose with their DJ, Spinderella.
Spinderella was in high school when she joined the group.**

rhyme on it. So the two women wrote a rap called "Show Stopper." It was an "answer song." It answered "The Show." That was a rap by Doug E. Fresh and Slick Rick.

"Show Stopper" was really good. So Cheryl and Sandra formed a group. It was called Salt-N-Pepa. Later, they got a high-school student to be their DJ. She was called Spinderella.

Salt-N-Pepa made their first album in 1986. By 1988, they had sold more than a million records!

In 1989, the group was up for a Grammy Award. It was the first year that special Grammys were given out for rap.

But Salt-N-Pepa did not go to the awards show. Some Grammys were handed out on TV. But the rap Grammy was not. The people who ran the show didn't think anyone cared about seeing rappers on TV.

Salt-N-Pepa didn't think that was right. "If they don't want us, we don't want them," they said. The band stayed home from the show. (They didn't win, by the way.)

Today, the rap Grammys are on TV. Salt-N-Pepa helped make that happen.

They also led the way for other female rappers. Lil' Kim and Missy Elliot can thank Salt-N-Pepa for opening doors.

Should Salt-N-Pepa have gone to the Grammys? Why or why not?

Glossary

break dancing *(noun)* a kind of dancing done during drum breaks

lyrics *(noun)* words to a song

rhythms *(noun)* the repeated beats in music

spin *(verb)* to play

turntables *(noun)* record players

wired *(verb)* hooked up to electricity